Lord Cornwallis

British General

Colonial Leaders

Lord Baltimore
English Politician and Colonist

Benjamin Banneker
American Mathematician and Astronomer

Sir William Berkeley
Governor of Virginia

William Bradford
Governor of Plymouth Colony

Jonathan Edwards
Colonial Religious Leader

Benjamin Franklin
American Statesman, Scientist, and Writer

Anne Hutchinson
Religious Leader

Cotton Mather
Author, Clergyman, and Scholar

Increase Mather
Clergyman and Scholar

James Oglethorpe
Humanitarian and Soldier

William Penn
Founder of Democracy

Sir Walter Raleigh
English Explorer and Author

Caesar Rodney
American Patriot

John Smith
English Explorer and Colonist

Miles Standish
Plymouth Colony Leader

Peter Stuyvesant
Dutch Military Leader

George Whitefield
Clergyman and Scholar

Roger Williams
Founder of Rhode Island

John Winthrop
Politician and Statesman

John Peter Zenger
Free Press Advocate

Revolutionary War Leaders

John Adams
Second U.S. President

Samuel Adams
Patriot

Ethan Allen
Revolutionary Hero

Benedict Arnold
Traitor to the Cause

John Burgoyne
British General

George Rogers Clark
American General

Lord Cornwallis
British General

Thomas Gage
British General

King George III
English Monarch

Nathanael Greene
Military Leader

Nathan Hale
Revolutionary Hero

Alexander Hamilton
First U.S. Secretary of the Treasury

John Hancock
President of the Continental Congress

Patrick Henry
American Statesman and Speaker

William Howe
British General

John Jay
First Chief Justice of the Supreme Court

Thomas Jefferson
Author of the Declaration of Independence

John Paul Jones
Father of the U.S. Navy

Thaddeus Kosciuszko
Polish General and Patriot

Lafayette
French Freedom Fighter

James Madison
Father of the Constitution

Francis Marion
The Swamp Fox

James Monroe
American Statesman

Thomas Paine
Political Writer

Molly Pitcher
Heroine

Paul Revere
American Patriot

Betsy Ross
American Patriot

Baron Von Steuben
American General

George Washington
First U.S. President

Anthony Wayne
American General

Famous Figures of the Civil War Era

John Brown
Abolitionist

Jefferson Davis
Confederate President

Frederick Douglass
Abolitionist and Author

Stephen A. Douglas
Champion of the Union

David Farragut
Union Admiral

Ulysses S. Grant
Military Leader and President

Stonewall Jackson
Confederate General

Joseph E. Johnston
Confederate General

Robert E. Lee
Confederate General

Abraham Lincoln
Civil War President

George Gordon Meade
Union General

George McClellan
Union General

William Henry Seward
Senator and Statesman

Philip Sheridan
Union General

William Sherman
Union General

Edwin Stanton
Secretary of War

Harriet Beecher Stowe
Author of Uncle Tom's Cabin

James Ewell Brown Stuart
Confederate General

Sojourner Truth
Abolitionist, Suffragist, and Preacher

Harriet Tubman
Leader of the Underground Railroad

Lord Cornwallis

British General

Daniel E. Harmon

Arthur M. Schlesinger, jr.
Senior Consulting Editor

Chelsea House Publishers

Philadelphia

CHELSEA HOUSE PUBLISHERS
Editor-in-Chief Sally Cheney
Director of Production Kim Shinners
Production Manager Pamela Loos
Art Director Sara Davis
Production Editor Diann Grasse

Staff for *LORD CORNWALLIS*
Editor Sally Cheney
Associate Art Director Takeshi Takahashi
Series Design Keith Trego
Cover Design 21st Century Publishing and Communications, Inc.
Picture Researcher Pat Holl
Layout 21st Century Publishing and Communications, Inc.

The Chelsea House World Wide Web address is
http://www.chelseahouse.com

First Printing
1 3 5 7 9 8 6 4 2

Library of Congress Cataloging-in-Publication Data

Harmon, Daniel E.
    Lord Cornwallis / Daniel E. Harmon.
        p. cm. — (Revolutionary War leaders)
    Includes bibliographical references and index.
    ISBN 0-7910-6396-8 (hc : alk. paper) — ISBN 0-7910-6397-6
    (pbk. : alk. paper)
      1. Cornwallis, Charles Cornwallis, Marquis, 1738-1805—Juvenile
    literature. 2. Generals—Great Britain—Biography—Juvenile litera-
    ture. 3. United States—History—Revolution, 1775-1783—British
    forces—Juvenile literature. 4. United States—History—Revolution,
    1775-1783—Campaigns—Juvenile literature. [1. Cornwallis,
    Charles Cornwallis, Marquis, 1738-1805. 2. Generals. 3. United
    States—History—Revolution, 1775-1783.] I. Title. II. Series.

DA67.1.C77 H37 2001
941.07'3'092—dc21
    [B]   2001028525

Contents

1 A Young Nobleman
Joins the Army   7

2 Family Man and
Army General   17

3 Chasing the Americans   29

4 Bad News from
the Colonies   43

5 Trapped at Yorktown   53

6 From Defeat to Victory   65

Glossary   72

Chronology   74

Revolutionary War
Time Line   75

Further Reading   77

Index   78

The Thames River runs through London. The river was important to England as a source of drinking water and as a way to transport goods. Several bridges connect the northern and southern parts of London.

A Young Nobleman Joins the Army

Charles Cornwallis was born in eastern England on December 31, 1738. He became the second Earl Cornwallis (his father was the first). One day Charles would become a respected British army commander. Sadly, he's best known today not for his title or his cleverness in war, but for surrendering his army at Yorktown, Virginia, in the American Revolution.

His ancestors were wealthy, respected landowners. Centuries earlier, one of them had been a sheriff of London. They lived at Brome Hall in the county of Suffolk, England. That's how Charles' got his childhood title: Lord Brome.

One of his uncles held the important title of archbishop of Canterbury. His mother, too, came from a well-respected family. Sir Robert Walpole, a prime minister of England, was her uncle.

Before he was old enough for schooling, Lord Brome learned to ride horses. Soon he was joining other upper class men and boys in the popular–and slightly dangerous–horseback sport of the time: fox hunting. He also learned to shoot a gun as a child. He brought to the kitchen many a pheasant and other tasty game fowl.

His family sent him to Eton. This is a famous, time-honored boarding school where many of England's statesmen, military commanders, writers, and other leaders were educated. Lord Brome, like other students of his social standing, lived in rooms off the school campus. This was one way the youngsters of nobility and wealth set themselves apart themselves from the "common" students who lived on campus.

But being wealthy didn't mean life was easy for

Charles attended Eton, a well-known boarding school that educated many of England's military and government leaders.

Lord Brome and the other students from noble families. Their teachers, or masters, physically beat them if they fell behind in their studies. Students treated one another sternly, often violently. They played brutal games that sometimes broke bones and, more than once, resulted in death. Lord Brome once was hit in the eye with a field hockey stick, leaving a blemish that would last the rest of his life.

Young Charles had a well-rounded upbringing. He learned to enjoy literature and art and the fine things of English society. But he also learned to survive Eton, a "school of hard knocks" if ever there was one. This combination of a sensitive mind and strong body would serve him well in the future.

Many teenage boys of his social class went to one of England's distinguished universities—and so did Charles, enrolling at Clare College, Cambridge. Afterward, he could have become a lawyer, a church leader, a public official, or a member of **Parliament**. But for the long term, Lord Brome had his heart set on another calling, one of adventure and glory.

During the 18th century, England often was at war—usually against France. For well-bred young men like Lord Brome, an attractive career to pursue was in the royal army or navy. He chose the army. He would be an officer, of course, not a front-line soldier. This was the privilege of upper-class young men. When he was only 17, he was given a **commission** as a junior officer in Britain's 1st Grenadier Guards.

Charles took his profession quite seriously. He knew that because of his family's position, he probably could avoid participating in dangerous battles, and still rise in rank over the years. Rather than take the easy course, though, he decided to learn all he could about warfare and become the best officer he could be.

He was especially eager to study infantry and cavalry **tactics**. England at the time had no special military schools, or academies, devoted to those branches of the army. So Charles went to the city of Turin in present-day Italy, which had one of Europe's finest military academies. His tutor and family friend, Captain de Roguin, went with him.

At Turin, Charles learned not only the art of

war, but also the art of high society. Besides mathematics, German, and military studies, he was given formal teaching in ballroom dancing. He regularly attended operas and visited the court of the King of Sardinia twice a week.

After a few months, he and de Roguin left Turin and toured Europe. They were in Geneva, Switzerland, when Charles learned that his regiment at home, the 1st Grenadier Guards, had been ordered to join England's German allies on the European mainland. The German provinces, or states, feared they were about to be **invaded** by France and Austria. England promised Germany aid.

Charles was dismayed. How he yearned to be with his regiment, preparing for war. But he could not reach them before they set out on their mission.

As events would prove, he was in the right place at the right time after all. He volunteered for service under German Prince Ferdinand of Brunswick. Less than two months later, in

August 1758, a British force led by the Marquis of Granby joined Ferdinand's army. The 19-year-old Charles was appointed camp assistant to Granby.

For the next four years, he gained a valuable military education on the battlegrounds of Europe. This conflict, which had begun in 1756, would be known to history as the Seven Years' War. On one side were England, Prussia, and Hanover (two German states). On the other were France, Austria, Russia, Sweden, Saxony, and Spain. The gaily colored armies maneuvered across Europe. They also fought in Quebec (Canada) and India.

Eventually, England and Prussia would score the most gains. England, for example, expanded its **colonies**—the territories under its control overseas. One unhappy result for the British was that 15 years later, its old enemy France, stung by this defeat, would join the American freedom fighters in the Revolution.

In 1759, Charles was promoted to captain. Two

THE THIRTEEN COLONIES
IN 1775

Scale of miles

100   50   0   100   200

Extent of Settlement

**This map shows the 13 British colonies in
America as they looked in 1775.**

years later, he was made commander of a regiment and given the rank of lieutenant-colonel.

The young officer distinguished himself

across Germany during the war. He acquired not just military skills, but confidence, courage, and physical strength. He knew this was what he was meant to do with his life.

The war ended early and sadly for Lord Brome. In July 1762, he received word of his father's death. It was his duty now to return to England and his family. He inherited his father's title of nobility and duties of public service. Lord Brome became Earl Cornwallis. He took his father's seat in the House of Lords, one of the bodies of Parliament in London.

Without notice, the energetic soldier had been removed from the battlefield and cast into the role of English statesman. He was confident that in time, though, he would return to the army.

British troops arrived in New Jersey in November 1776.
Charles was defeated in New Jersey at the battle of Trenton
on December 26, 1776, and at Princeton on January 3, 1777.

2

Family Man and Army General

It was a challenge filling his father's place as head of a noble family and member of Parliament. Much responsibility suddenly had fallen on the shoulders of the young Lord Cornwallis. Despite the demands, though, Charles made time for enjoyment and romance.

Pretty Jemima Tullekin Jones became the love of his life. Her father was an army officer. Unlike Charles, however, she did not come from a famous or wealthy family. Because of that, their match was a bit unusual among Britain's upper class.

Their love for each other won out over social

standing, though. They were married in 1768 and settled at Brome Hall. Soon, they had one son, also named Charles, and one daughter, who they named Mary.

Lord Cornwallis was very busy. He divided his time between his quiet country home and busy London, where Parliament met.

Although he was one of the younger members of Parliament, Charles was not afraid to state his opinions about British government activities. For one thing, he did not share some of the other lords' disrespect for the American colonists, who had begun to resist English taxes. Charles voted against laws like the Stamp Act of 1765–one of the British actions that eventually caused the colonists to rebel.

This put him on the opposite side of the American argument from King George III. The king insisted that the colonists obey all the English laws and support the crown. The king was not angry at Charles personally, though. Rather, the two men got along well. King George recognized Charles as a fine military officer who one day

Colonists rioted against the British in response to the Stamp Act of 1765. The stamp had to be put on printed documents and served as a way for the king to collect taxes.

might be of very important service to England.

Britain began building up its troop force in America to put down any threat of violence by the unhappy settlers. Charles at this time expressed doubt that the king's forces could win an all-out war across the Atlantic. Later, after leading British armies successfully during the

King George III expected the American colonists to follow the laws and pay the taxes imposed by Great Britain. As the colonists rebelled, King George depended on officers such as Charles to fight in the colonies.

early fighting, he would change his mind.

That war began in April 1775. The first shots of the American Revolution were fired in the Massachusetts colony. England responded by sending more soldiers and commanders to New England. Charles did not approve of the war, but he felt it was his duty to obey his king's wishes.

In early 1776, Charles was made a general in the army. He was ordered to go with 2,500 soldiers by ship to the port of Charleston, South Carolina. There he was to help a senior British commander, General Henry Clinton, capture the city from the Americans.

The operation against Charleston failed. British marines could not storm the beaches in great force because of sandbars and tidal holes along the surf bottom. Broadsides of cannonballs fired from their ships did not destroy the American forts that over-looked Charleston Harbor. Meanwhile, American gunners from the shore pummeled the British ships with deadly cannon fire. More than 200 **redcoats**–many of them officers–were killed or wounded. The great English assault force had to stand off into the open sea. Several weeks later, they set a course far up the coast for New York.

Clinton, not Charles, had to bear the criticism

When they tried to capture Charleston, South Carolina, in 1776, the British were not prepared to find several peculiar obstacles in their way.

First was the entrance to Charleston Harbor with its sandy islands. The **Patriots** held forts overlooking the harbor and had cannons aimed at the British fleet as it sailed near. When British soldiers entered the shallow waters to storm the forts, they stepped into deep holes under the water, created by tidal currents. Sandbars stopped the British row boats as they got near the shore.

So the British decided to pull back their marines and simply bombard the forts with their ships' heavy cannons until the Americans surrendered. But the rebels had built their fort walls out of local palmetto logs. This type of wood is soft and spongy. The British gunners aimed accurately and hit the fort walls many times—but to their astonishment, the walls did not shatter apart as they expected. Instead, their cannonballs were embedded harmlessly into the soft logs and the sand that was piled behind them.

for retreating from Charleston. A letter believed to have been written by a government official in London expressed sympathy for Charles: "A man such as Lord Cornwallis never should have been sent to Charleston. He's far too good a soldier for such a puny operation. Now that he is free to move into the middle colonies, we shall hear from him again soon, and rebels will be whistling out of the other side of their mouths."

Later in the Revolution, Charles again would have General Clinton as his commanding officer. They got along but were not close friends. Both were generals, and both wanted to be in charge. Clinton was a jealous commander, afraid Charles or another officer under him would rise to take his place. Charles, for his part, was eager to command a force distant from General Clinton so he could make his own decisions.

Clinton had to make himself exactly clear whenever he gave Charles orders. If not, Charles might take Clinton's commands to mean what he wanted them to mean—not what Clinton really intended. This competition between the two men eventually would lead to disaster for the British in America.

In summer 1776, after failing to capture the port of Charleston, Charles arrived in New York Harbor. There he joined a massive force commanded by British General William Howe. Some 32,000 British and **Hessian** soldiers were assembled— the biggest army England ever had sent to fight in a foreign country. They were very well trained, and they were eager to crush the rebellious

General George Washington was forced to retreat at Long Island, New York, in August 1776. British General William Howe's troops were more experienced than the American soldiers.

yankees of the American colonies.

For the next six months, it seemed they indeed would crush them. After taking Long Island, New York, and other important places, they began driving George Washington's ragged, starving American forces across New Jersey.

It appeared Charles' early worries about England's military success in America were pointless.

Charles led the British forces pursuing George Washington's American army in late 1776. Only the coming of winter interrupted the chase. As snow and ice cast their frozen spell over the northern colonies, the redcoats settled into warm winter quarters, while Washington struggled to keep his pitiful army together. Many American soldiers had been wounded, killed, or captured. Others had deserted, convinced the Revolution could not succeed. Washington's army that once numbered 20,000 men was reduced to about 3,000. He was able to muster a few **reinforcements**, but they were no match for the British and Hessian hordes.

While the British army set up lodgings in towns along the east bank of the Delaware River, Charles thought he might sail home to England for the winter. He missed his wife. He saw no reason why he shouldn't enjoy the warm fires and comforts of his family home, while the American rebels shivered in the New Jersey snow. At any rate, there would be no more fighting for a few months—or so he thought.

Then Washington performed his famous, heroic

miracle of the war. He moved his desperate army across the Delaware River on Christmas night 1776 and captured a sleeping Hessian force at Trenton, New Jersey. Washington then made Trenton his own headquarters.

Receiving word of the shocking setback, Charles forgot his plans to return to England. He marched on Trenton with a large army. They arrived late in the day January 2, 1777, and prepared to storm General Washington's position the next morning.

Some of Charles's officers wanted to attack the Americans immediately, before darkness fell. Charles decided not to; the troops were too tired from their hurried march. The morning, he reasoned, would be soon enough to get their revenge for Trenton and possibly end the war. "The fox," as he nicknamed Washington, was about to be caught.

But the British approached an empty town the next day. Washington's army had slipped away during the night. The American commander had ordered his men to tie rags around the wheels of their **artillery** pieces to dull their loud clatter. A small

British ships are shown here as they enter the harbor in New York City. Fort George and the city are shown in the background.

detachment had stayed in Trenton and created a great deal of noise, banging on pots around the campfires. The British, listening through the darkness, thought the American army was preparing for battle. In reality, most of Washington's soldiers were moving away toward Princeton, New Jersey.

It was not the last time George Washington would "out-fox" Charles Cornwallis.

Hessian troops from the British army surrendered to George Washington after the Battle of Trenton, New Jersey.

3

Chasing the Americans

After escaping from Charles's army at Trenton, New Jersey, in January 1777, George Washington proved to be a dangerous opponent. His American army defeated a smaller British force before Charles and his men could turn and catch up to them.

But both armies were exhausted. They stopped fighting and went into winter quarters to wait for spring to thaw the frozen rivers and hard dirt roads.

Their victory at Trenton had breathed life into the ragged, half-starved Patriots. Charles and the

General Cornwallis's best field officer was also his most hated by the Americans. Lieutenant Colonel Banastre Tarleton was called the "Green **Dragoon**" by his friends (because his soldiers wore green jackets), and "Bloody Ban" by his foes. He commanded a Tory horseback unit known as the British Legion.

"These miserable Americans must be taught their places," Tarleton insisted to his fellow officers. He demonstrated this at the Battle of Waxhaws, South Carolina. When his opponent, Colonel Abraham Buford, waved a white flag and tried to surrender, Tarleton ignored the signal until his men had slaughtered more than a hundred Americans who were laying down their arms.

After surrendering with the British army at Yorktown in 1781, Tarleton was hardly punished for his ruthless wartime actions. Instead, he went back to England, became a member of Parliament, was knighted by King George IV, and eventually was promoted to the rank of general in the army.

other British leaders pursued them grimly during the next three years. During this time, Charles showed his talents as an army commander especially well at the battles of Brandywine Creek, Pennsylvania (September 1777) and Monmouth Courthouse, New Jersey (June 1778). After being embarrassed by "the fox" at Trenton, Charles had recovered his reputation. He had proved his value as one of the king's best officers in America.

Then he returned to England. His wife Jemima was very sick.

(Some of her friends believed she was broken-hearted because of Charles's long absence across the sea.) She died soon after the new year began.

Charles grieved terribly. Jemima's death, he told a relative, "destroyed all my hopes of happiness in this world." Brome Hall now was an empty, painful place to him, not the lovely country retreat it always had been. What could he do to pull himself out of his depression?

He could return to the army. He must do what he could to help end the long, bloody war across the Atlantic and establish British control securely in the colonies. So Charles was back in America in August 1779.

Some historians believe if he hadn't been so distressed by Jemima's death, Charles never would have returned to America. He knew he probably never would be named the overall British commander there—although he possibly was the best British general in the colonies. The best he could look forward to was getting command of one of several British armies assigned to different parts of America. He only went back to the colonies to forget his deep sorrow.

Charles and his fellow British commanders watched the Patriots grow bolder, wiser, and more determined than ever to win independence from England. It became harder and harder for the proud British to gain clear victories. Even when the Americans suffered more losses than the British in a battle, the rebels were taking one more step toward winning the war. That was because England, with territories to guard all over the globe, could not afford to lose any soldiers at all. More and more American colonists, meanwhile, were being persuaded to join the fight for freedom.

That wasn't the only problem for the redcoats in America. France, England's long-time enemy, by now had joined the Revolution on the side of the Patriots. It sent armies to serve under Washington's command. It also sent supplies, and it dispatched naval fleets to harass the Royal Navy off the American coast and in the West Indies islands. In England, a growing number of people–including members of Parliament–wanted to stop pouring money into the war effort, give up the American colonies, and bring their soldiers home.

In late 1779, the British high command decided to send a large army from the northern colonies back to the Carolinas. If they could soundly defeat the lower colonies, they now believed, it would be only a short time until the northern colonies surrendered, as well. The frustrating war would finally be over.

General Henry Clinton led this force of about 8,000 soldiers. After a rough voyage down the coast, they arrived by ship in the seaport of Charleston, South Carolina, in February 1780. The city was still in American hands. Charles was second in command under Clinton.

The British army surrounded and bombarded the port. Soon, the Patriot commander, Benjamin Lincoln, surrendered his army of more than 5,000. It was one of the worst American defeats in the war. With Charleston captured, it appeared the war in the southern colonies soon would be over.

In June, Clinton returned to New York, and Charles took over the British command in the Carolinas. The next month, the American Congress appointed General Horatio Gates commander of the Patriots in the south. Gates was no match for Charles and the experienced British soldiers.

Charles proved this quickly at the Battle of Camden on August 16. The British easily caused Gates's larger American army to retreat. In one quick action, the American army in the south, left weakened after the fall of Charleston, was almost totally destroyed.

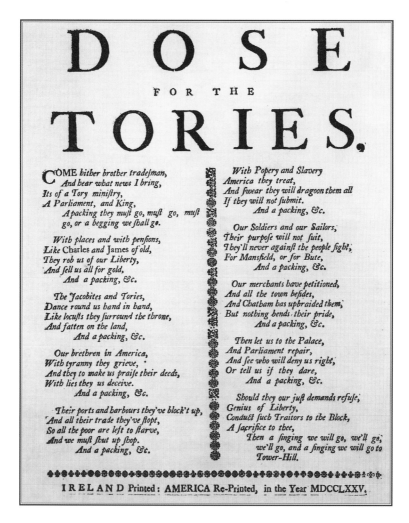

DOSE
FOR THE
TORIES.

COME hither brother tradesman,
And hear what news I bring,
Its of a Tory ministry,
A Parliament, and King,
    A packing they must go, must go, must
    go, or a begging we shall go.

With places and with pensions,
Like Charles and James of old,
They rob us of our Liberty,
And sell us all for gold,
    And a packing, &c.

The Jacobites and Tories,
Dance round us hand in hand,
Like locusts they surround the throne,
And fatten on the land,
    And a packing, &c.

Our brethren in America,
With tyranny they grieve,
And they to make us praise their deeds,
With lies they us deceive.
    And a packing, &c.

Their ports and harbours they've block't up,
And all their trade they've stopt,
So all the poor are left to starve,
And we must shut up shop.
    And a packing, &c.

With Popery and Slavery
America they treat,
And swear they will dragoon them all
If they will not submit.
    And a packing, &c.

Our Soldiers and our Sailors,
Their purpose will not suit,
They'll never against the people fight,
For Mansfield, or for Bute,
    And a packing, &c.

Our merchants have petitioned,
And all the town besides,
And Chatham has upbraided them,
But nothing bends their pride,
    And a packing, &c.

Then let us to the Palace,
And Parliament repair,
And see who will deny us right,
Or tell us if they dare,
    And a packing, &c.

Should they our just demands refuse,
Genius of Liberty,
Conduct such Traitors to the Block,
A sacrifice to thee,
    Then a singing we will go, we'll go,
    we'll go, and a singing we will go to
    Tower-Hill.

IRELAND Printed: AMERICA Re-Printed, in the Year MDCCLXXV.

This broadside is a poem criticizing the Tories, who were colonists that supported the continuation of British rule in America.

The British military leaders, including Charles, believed it would be easy to bring the southern part of the Revolution to an end now. Charles found valuable help among the colonists themselves. More than a few Carolina planters–like many townspeople in the north and settlers on the frontier–felt they owed their allegiance to King George, not to the Patriot cause.

These supporters, called **Loyalists** or **Tories**, sometimes went to extremes in fighting their Patriot neighbors. They brutally ambushed and killed many Carolina **civilians** who favored independence–prompting the Patriots to do the same against the Loyalists. Many historians have called this America's first "civil war," because neighbors, old friends, and in some instances, close relatives fought against one another.

But for better or worse, Tories helped the British regulars win many battles and *skirmishes*– short-lived clashes involving small groups of fighters.

In the south, skirmishes were more frequent than fully pitched battles. Patriot leaders like

Lieutenant Colonel Francis Marion, Andrew Pickens, and Thomas Sumter kept Charles' forces occupied with surprise raids against their South Carolina outposts and supply lines. British cavalry and foot soldiers replied by scouring the countryside, looking for Patriots and sometimes burning their family farms.

A major battle was in the making, however. In early October, the British stirred up an unexpected problem on the Carolina frontier.

Charles sent a band of more than 1,000 Tories on a sweep through the west of the colonies to stamp out pockets of resistance. They were led by an excellent British officer, Major Patrick Ferguson. Their movements alarmed the settlers living in the Smoky Mountains and beyond. The local farmers and hunters knew the redcoats' reputation for burning and ruining colonists' farms and towns to the east and north. Was Ferguson coming to sack their pioneer homesteads, too?

Major Patrick Ferguson, the British commander who lost the Battle of King's Mountain in 1780, was both "an officer and a gentleman." In fact, his kindness on one occasion may have greatly helped the Americans win the Revolution by sparing the life of General George Washington.

Three years before, at the Battle of Brandywine Creek, Pennsylvania, Ferguson had the great American commander in his rifle sight. Washington was sitting atop his horse, his back turned to Ferguson's position.

As a hunter in private life, Ferguson only shot at birds in flight, never at birds perched on tree limbs or fences. At Brandywine, he felt the situation was the same. "It would not be gentlemanly to shoot a man in the back of the head," he stated, deciding not to pull the trigger.

At King's Mountain, Ferguson was killed by American frontier riflemen.

About 900 eagle-eyed riflemen, known to history as the "over-mountain men," came together from what is now western North Carolina and eastern Tennessee. They attacked Ferguson's force at King's Mountain, a long, low peak just below the South/North Carolina border. Shooting from behind rocks and trees, they inched their way toward the Tory position along the summit. The Tories were surrounded, Ferguson was killed, and the British frontier force was almost totally wiped out.

Charles was shocked. He had thought

defeating the Carolina colonies, already weakened and discouraged by 1780, would be easy. Now, he realized, he had a real fight on his hands.

He soon had a real enemy leader on his hands, as well. By now, it was plain to the continental government that bumbling, timid General Gates was not an effective battle commander. Congress told General Washington to replace Gates with a new southern leader. Washington's choice: the cautious but brilliant Major General Nathanael Greene.

Greene had been a vital, effective commander in Washington's northern campaigns. He never had won a great victory–but he knew how to steal it cleverly from the grasp of the enemy, escaping without crippling losses among his troops. He was skillful at fending off powerful foes and using his time wisely.

The new American leader arrived in Charlotte, North Carolina, in early December 1780. Though heavily outnumbered by

**Major General Nathanael Greene was
appointed by George Washington to lead
the southern army.**

Charles's forces, Greene had some excellent
ideas for using the few strengths his Patriots
possessed. The British soon would experience

more defeat. Even when British forces won the day in battle, it would cost them more deaths and injuries than England could afford to pay for victory.

Lieutenant Colonel William Washington led the American cavalry to victory at the Battle at the Cowpens, South Carolina.

Bad News from the Colonies

Lord Cornwallis was in a very dark mood as he took up his pen. "The late affair," he scrawled in a letter to a fellow British officer, Lord Francis Rawdon, "has almost broke my heart. . . . I was never more surrounded with difficulty and distress. . . ."

It was January 1781, more than five years into the American Revolution. "The late affair" was the British loss at the Battle of Cowpens, South Carolina.

Charles himself never appeared on the frozen foothills pasture called "Hannah's Cowpens" near the border dividing the two Carolina colonies. His young cavalry commander, Banastre Tarleton, led the redcoats there.

Tarleton was perhaps England's finest cavalry officer. A bold, gifted leader, Tarleton should have won at Cowpens, Charles believed. Instead, his horse soldier was outwitted by crafty Daniel Morgan, who commanded a ragtag, half-starved force of frontier sharpshooters and hardened Patriot regulars. Some of the Americans didn't have shoes, much less uniforms to match those of Tarleton's fine British soldiers.

American cavalry leader, Lieutenant Colonel William Washington attacked Tarleton at Cowpens. After a few sabre slashes—none finding their mark—Tarleton dashed away, shooting Washington's horse from under him.

Charles blamed Tarleton's men, not their commander, for the loss. He wrote Tarleton a nice letter expressing his sympathy for the way the battled ended.

It did not mean the Americans had won the war. Both Lord Cornwallis and Tarleton would fight again. The British no longer controlled the course of the war in the south, though. From now on, they had to plan their movements according to the movements of American commander Nathanael Greene.

This was maddening to Charles. He had a much larger army than Greene, yet Greene was able to decide where and when they would fight.

At that point, Charles felt the most important thing to do was chase down and destroy Greene, Morgan, and their small but dangerous army. Charles was furious at the Cowpens disaster. By the time he received word of the defeat and set his army in motion, though, the Americans were well on their way north, moving through central North Carolina toward the Virginia border. To some southern colonists, it appeared the American commander was abandoning them to the enraged British and Tories. Greene knew, however, that Charles also would abandon the British head-quarters and outposts in South Carolina in order to pursue him.

Charles hoped to catch the Americans in North Carolina and score a decisive victory. If he could, the war in the lower colonies would be all but over. But Greene dodged him. The Patriots reached the Dan River, seized all the boats and ferries, and crossed into Virginia. The British were left stranded on the southern shore, unable to follow.

Charles set up new headquarters in Hillsboro, North Carolina. There, he rested his army and summoned Loyalists living in the colony to join him. He knew Greene would come back to fight.

Indeed, small, swift-striking American units soon crossed the river into North Carolina, raiding Tory strongholds and capturing British supplies. In March, Greene arrived with his main army at a hilltop town called Guilford Court House.

The British went to meet him. They rushed fearlessly into the American lines, up a hill toward the courthouse. For a moment it seemed the determined British advance guards, commanded by General Charles O'Hara, would smash through Greene's army and deliver the final blow Charles so badly wanted. They actually reached the top of the hill and captured some of the American artillery.

Lieutenant Colonel Henry Lee, also called Lighthouse Harry Lee, and his cavalry attacked the British in the Carolinas. Lee's attacks allowed Nathanael Greene's army to retreat across North Carolina to Virginia.

Suddenly, they were stunned by a furious countercharge by veteran continental troops from Maryland and Delaware. Then they were hit by a sabre-wielding American cavalry force. The hill now swarmed with a tangle of many-colored uniforms. The scene was so confusing that officers found it difficult to organize the men under their commands, either to attack or retreat.

Charles later described Guilford Court House as the most violent battle he'd ever seen. Watching the hopeless struggle from a distance, he made a difficult decision that astounded some of his own officers: He ordered his artillery to bombard the hill. American and British soldiers alike were killed in the dreadful cannon fire.

The harsh tactic broke apart the stalled battle. The Americans straggled back, and Greene withdrew his army from Guilford Court House. Redcoats occupied the hill—but they were so exhausted they couldn't follow the enemy.

Charles's "victory" at Guilford Court House did nothing to help win the war. In fact, so many of his men were killed and wounded—twice as many as the Patriots—that he knew in his heart it was really a defeat. His army was suffering many losses. Greene's Americans, meanwhile, appeared as determined as ever to resist.

Back in England, an unhappy member of Parliament, Charles James Fox, remarked, "A few more such victories would destroy the British Army."

The frustrated Charles decided to relocate his army to the North Carolina coast. There they could regroup, rest, and repair and replace damaged and lost equipment.

He would forget his desire to crush Nathanael Greene in the Carolinas. Sir Henry Clinton, the overall British commander based in New York, wanted to launch a massive attack against the colony of Virginia.

Throughout the war, Virginia had not seen as much fighting as most of the other colonies. Leaders in London had thought the northern colonies and the Carolinas were the most important areas to control. Now, however, they realized the Patriots were able to raise much of the money to buy their equipment and supplies by selling tobacco to foreign countries. Virginia and the Chesapeake Bay were the center of this trade. Supply ships entered and

Benedict Arnold was a brilliant army commander. His bold, daring leadership in the face of devastating rifle and cannon fire was one of the reasons the Americans defeated and captured a whole British army near Saratoga, New York, in 1777. He was an American hero then—but he would end the war as a hated traitor to the American cause.

Arnold resented the American Congress because its key leaders passed over him in choosing the Continental Army's top officers. Although Arnold was among the best and bravest, he watched as Congress gave higher commands to weak generals who were friends of the politicians. In 1780, after marrying a Tory woman, Arnold sold his services to the British. He led raids against the Americans in Virginia and New England near the end of the war.

Later leaving the colonies to live in England, Arnold found himself scorned by British society. Although he had joined their side in the Revolution, the people in England had little respect for traitors in any uniform. Arnold died a poor man in London in 1801.

departed the colonies by slipping up the Chesapeake to Baltimore, then back down and onto the open Atlantic. If the British established a powerful army and navy base on the Chesapeake, they could choke the Patriots' flow of supplies.

Already, a redcoat force under Benedict Arnold—the American traitor who once had been one of the Patriots' finest commanders—was based in Portsmouth. This was in the "Tidewater" region of the lower Virginia coast. Clinton was sending several thousand more soldiers there.

Benedict Arnold

Charles took 1,500 of his own men to join them.
When he arrived, Charles would be in command
of this huge new army.

So he turned his attention far up the coast,
toward a place called Yorktown.

The Marquis de Lafayette was a French commander who joined in the American's fight for independence.

Trapped at Yorktown

hen Charles decided to move up to Virginia, he was not exactly obeying the wishes of his superior commander. General Clinton wanted him to completely conquer the Carolina colonies before coming north. Instead, Charles left a strong British force behind him in the Carolinas—but he also left Nathanael Greene's Americans on the prowl.

Charles, though, believed that if the British could overrun Virginia, the Carolinas would be cut off from the other colonies. Then they easily would fall; hardly any more fighting would be necessary there. But he believed it was pointless to try to conquer the Carolinas until Virginia was brought firmly under British control.

In their letters to each other, the two men squabbled for months. Clinton had the authority to tell Charles what to do, but Charles often managed to get his way.

In May 1781, Charles and his men arrived in Virginia. There, he found himself in command of a mighty army numbering more than 7,000 soldiers. Against them were only 3,000 Americans led by the Marquis de Lafayette, a French commander who was helping the Americans, and General Anthony Wayne. The British should be able to defeat them quickly, Charles thought.

However, Lafayette–like Greene–proved too clever to be caught and beaten. His men would skirmish with the British, then withdraw; and repeat the pattern. The Americans knew they could not defeat Charles's army, but they kept the British off-balance.

Meanwhile, Clinton in New York was worried.

Anthony Wayne and his men fought the British in Savannah, Georgia, in July 1782.

He was afraid George Washington's army in the north might attack him. He nervously ordered Charles to ship him 3,000 men as reinforcements; then he ordered the reinforcements to stay in Virginia. Unsure what Washington planned to do,

Clinton could not make up his mind. Finally, he told Charles to establish a base for the British navy on the Virginia coast. They chose Yorktown for the site, a port near the mouth of the York River.

Throughout the summer, the warring armies skirmished. Clinton dueled against Washington and Comte de Rochambeau (another French commander fighting for America) in New York. Charles faced Lafayette and Wayne in Virginia. No decisive battles were fought. But far across the ocean, in a group of islands called the West Indies, a decision was being made that would affect the outcome of the war.

England and France had been fierce rivals for centuries. Not surprisingly, France was siding with the colonists against Great Britain in the American Revolution. Besides sending army commanders like Lafayette and Rochambeau to aid George Washington on the mainland, the French sent a fleet of warships, with transport vessels carrying several thousand soldiers, to harass the British-held West Indies. This French fleet was commanded

Comte de Grasse commanded a fleet of French
warships that were sent to work against the
British in the West Indies.

by Comte François Joseph Paul de Grasse.

Washington and Rochambeau sent couriers
by ship to ask de Grasse for help. He could
strike a more important blow against the British
in America, they persuaded him, than he could

in the islands. De Grasse at last agreed. He would bring his ships and soldiers to Virginia.

This was a golden opportunity for the Americans. Washington realized if he could get his own army down to Virginia to join Lafayette, and if de Grasse could arrive before British reinforcements, they could trap Charles at Yorktown.

By the time over-cautious Henry Clinton realized General Washington was not going to attack New York after all, Washington and Rochambeau were on their way to Virginia. Clinton was shocked and helpless. He knew he could not catch the southbound Americans overland because they'd gotten a head start. All he could do was wait for a British fleet to come and transport his army down the coast to assist Charles.

But it was too late for that desperate measure. Admiral de Grasse already had arrived in the Chesapeake Bay. He controlled the waters off Yorktown with a fleet powerful enough to block the British from entering.

When the Americans from the north joined

Lafayette's forces in September, Washington suddenly had an awesome, combined army of 16,000 soldiers—more than twice as many as Charles. The British commander was used to having the superior force in battle. Now he was woefully out-manned—and trapped. "If you cannot relieve me very soon," he warned Clinton in a letter, "you must be prepared to hear the worst."

With de Grasse cutting off any possible escape by sea, Charles saw but once chance: cross the York River and try to break through the American blockade at a place called Gloucester Point. The British had set up outposts there. From Gloucester Point, they might be able to escape northward along the Chesapeake.

But the Patriots were alert. They sent extra soldiers to the area. On October 3, an American-French force led by the Marquis de Choisy drove back a British thrust commanded by Banastre Tarleton. Patriots now controlled that side of the river.

Lord Cornwallis and Tarleton yearned for the

Carolinas. There, they had roamed and conquered freely, challenged only by small groups of scrappy, poorly equipped rebels. Now they were practically imprisoned. Attack was out of the question against an allied army so large.

Beginning October 9, French and American artillery bombarded the British at Yorktown day and night. Washington ordered trenches dug ever closer to the town. British **casualties** mounted. "We continue to lose men very fast," Charles wrote in a desperate letter to Clinton.

On the morning of October 17, Charles made the saddest decision of his life. He sent messengers to General Washington to make the best terms possible for an honorable surrender. Washington was hard to deal with. He refused the request that the British and Hessians be allowed to return immediately to England; rather, they would be placed in prisoner-of-war camps. Charles had no choice but to agree, or watch his army gradually be killed by rebel artillery. On October 19, 1781, he formally surrendered.

French and American artillery constantly bombarded the British at Yorktown, Virginia.

It was his darkest day. Lord Charles Cornwallis and his officers for six years had won more battles than they had lost. Now, he was surrendering almost the entire British southern army. In effect,

Lord Cornwallis did not know it, but on the day he surrendered at Yorktown, help was on the way. For many weeks, he had urged his superior general, Clinton, to send reinforcements from New York. Clinton had refused because he believed George Washington's Americans were going to attack New York, and Clinton needed his soldiers there.

After Clinton finally knew the truth—that Washington was marching on Yorktown, not New York—delays prevented him from sending a relief force to Charles right away. Finally, on October 17, 1781, a British fleet loaded with soldiers and supplies pulled up its anchors in New York Harbor and set sail for Yorktown. But as they took to the open sea, Charles' soldiers in Yorktown already were laying down their weapons.

he had lost the war for England—although most historians agree his superior officer, Clinton, was at least as much to blame for it as Charles.

When it came time for the ceremony of delivering his sword to the American commander, he could not bring himself to do it. Charles made the excuse that he was sick. He sent one of his officers, Brigadier General Charles O'Hara, instead. Then the British and Hessians marched somberly out of Yorktown and laid down their weapons.

His enemies sneered. So this was the mighty Cornwallis—refusing at

The American army set a trap for Charles at Yorktown. General Washington had 16,000 soldiers waiting there for Charles and his men.

the end to accept his defeat like a true soldier. Washington angrily refused to accept Charles's sword himself. He ordered O'Hara to hand it over to one of Washington's own subordinates, Brigadier General Benjamin Lincoln—the American commander who had surrendered Charleston to Clinton and Lord Cornwallis the year before.

Charles formally surrenders to George Washington on October 19, 1781, following the devastating British loss at Yorktown.

From Defeat to Victory

Charles had won great respect and honor as a young officer. Already, at 43, he had earned a place in world history. How could such a brilliant career fall to such a humiliating depth?

Charles had fought almost the entire American Revolution, in one colony or another. Yorktown was the only—and last—battle he ever personally lost in America. "I am quite tired of marching about the country in search of adventures," he wrote a fellow British general.

As thousands of redcoats and Germans marched out of Yorktown between lines of watchful American and British soldiers and laid down their arms, the British bands played a tune called "The World Turned Upside Down." Some of the defeated soldiers were crying. To Charles and his men, it seemed the world indeed had been turned topsy-turvy.

Lord North, the British prime minister, almost collapsed when he got word in London of the Yorktown defeat a month later. According to a witness, he took the news "as he would have taken a [musket] ball in his breast." Lord North shrieked, "Oh, God! It is all over!"

In France, diplomats received the word from a joyful Lafayette in America. "The play is over," the heroic leader announced. "The fifth act has come to an end."

But the Yorktown surrender did not quite end the Revolution. The British still held the southern seaports of Charleston and Savannah, as well as New York. Some Tories remained active, especially along the frontier. But they posed little threat. Most of the colonists now were free from King George's control. They were independent.

Most of Washington's men went home.

NORTH AMERICA
After the Treaty of 1783
Scale of miles

The Treaty of Paris was signed on September 3, 1783. The war was officially over, and three months later the last of the British troops left the United States.

The rest waited throughout 1782 as American, British, and French representatives bickered over terms of peace in Paris. Not until April 15, 1783, did Congress agree to a peace treaty. It was signed in Paris on September 3, almost two years after Charles's humiliation at Yorktown.

By then, Charles had returned to England. He was exchanged as a prisoner of war in May 1782 for captured American statesman Henry Laurens. Charles was received back home not as a downcast failure, but as a hero. The British people and Parliament believed Clinton, not Lord Cornwallis, was to blame for the loss at Yorktown. In an ongoing war of words, the two generals criticized each other's decisions and maneuvers for years.

Charles won that war. Clinton never again led a British army in battle and retired to a quiet life. For Charles, though, there were many more years of important tasks to perform for Great Britain.

In 1785, Charles was appointed England's representative to the court of the Prussian emperor. The following year, the government sent him to India to serve as **viceroy**, or ruler, of that large British colony. He was there seven years, directing the king's forces and taking steps to make the colonial government stronger and more effective.

He also was called on to fight. In 1790 a sultan in India rebelled against the British authorities. Charles led the king's forces in a careful campaign in 1791-92, trapping the sultan's rebels in a fortress. After Charles ordered an artillery attack, the sultan quickly surrendered. The king in England was so impressed by the way Charles handled the rebellion that he gave him the title of Marquis Cornwallis.

While in India, Charles badly missed his son, who like his father before him now bore the boyhood title "Lord Brome." The younger Cornwallis was at school in England. "I have rode once upon an elephant," Charles once wrote to his son, "but it is so like going in a cart, that you would not think it very agreeable."

In 1798, Charles was given the title of viceroy in Ireland. By that time, he had earned the respectful but demanding reputation as England's best military problem solver. When an uprising occurred in some part of the British Empire, the leaders in London knew Charles was the best commander for handling it.

In Ireland, France tried to help some of the people overthrow English rule that year. Charles and his troops put a stop to the attempt. At the same time, Charles was able to get along with most of the natives of Ireland. He managed the island's affairs for three years. He also served in the English cabinet as chief of defense matters.

Charles served as a British official in France in 1802, during the period when the French military commander Napoleon was waging wars across Europe and the Mediterranean region. Charles played a role in forming agreements to end some of the fighting.

Although he now was in his mid-60s, the British government needed Charles once more in India. He was appointed viceroy of the colony again in 1805. Charles didn't really want to go, but he felt it was his duty to England. This was the same attitude that had sent him to America, against his better judgment, in 1776.

He was in declining health. Soon after he

arrived back in India, while sailing up the Ganges River to meet with warring factions, he was stricken with a strange fever. Carried ashore, he died at a town called Ghazipur on October 5, 1805. He is buried near the great Ganges.

GLOSSARY

artillery–cannons, mortars, and other heavy guns in an army.

casualties–soldiers killed or injured in battle.

civilian–a person in wartime who is not a member of the armed forces.

colony–a foreign territory that a country controls and governs.

commission–in armies and navies of the 18th century, a government appointment of an officer to a particular rank.

dragoon–a heavily armed soldier on horseback.

Hessian–a soldier from the German state of Hesse who fought with England in the American Revolution.

invade–to send an army into a foreign land.

Loyalist–an American colonist who remained loyal to King George of England during the Revolution.

militia–a group of citizens who agree to arm themselves and fight for their country, state, or city in times of emergency, usually for only a short period of time.

Parliament–the British governing body, consisting of a House of Commons and House of Lords.

patriot–a person who faithfully supports his or her country even in times of trouble.

redcoats–common name for 18th-century British soldiers, most of whom wore bright red field jackets.

reinforcements–soldiers sent to help other soldiers in trouble, or sent from one part of a battlefield to help form a more powerful force in another area.

tactics–the ways in which a commander actually carries out a battle plan.

Tory–a supporter of England in the American colonies; also called a Loyalist.

viceroy–a person appointed to lead the government of a foreign colony.

CHRONOLOGY

1738	Charles Cornwallis is born in Suffolk County, England.
1755–1756	Becomes an officer in the 1st Grenadier Guards
1762	While fighting in the Seven Years' War in Europe, his father dies. He returns to England to succeed his father as Earl Cornwallis and take a seat in Parliament.
1768	Marries Jemima Tullekin Jones.
1776	Sent to fight in the American Revolution.
1777	General George Washington's army avoids capture by Charles's British and Hessian force in New Jersey and Pennsylvania.
1779	On the verge of retiring from the fighting in America, but grief over his wife's death prompts him to stay in the war.
1781	Surrounded by American and French forces, surrenders his army at Yorktown, Virginia, hastening the end of the American Revolution.
1786	Appointed viceroy of India, a British colony; later improves the colonial government and stops a native rebellion.
1798	Made viceroy of Britain's Irish colony and stops a rebellion backed by France.
1805	Arrives back in India for second appointment as viceroy; taken ill with a fever; and dies and is buried near the River Ganges.

REVOLUTIONARY WAR TIME LINE ═══

1765 The Stamp Act is passed by the British. Violent protests against it break out in the colonies.

1766 Britain ends the Stamp Act.

1767 Britain passes a law that taxes glass, painter's lead, paper, and tea in the colonies.

1770 Five colonists are killed by British soldiers in the Boston Massacre.

1773 People are angry about the taxes on tea. They throw boxes of tea from ships in Boston harbor into the water. It ruins the tea. The event is called the Boston Tea Party.

1774 The British pass laws to punish Boston for the Boston Tea Party. They close Boston harbor. Leaders in the colonies meet to plan a response to these actions.

1775 The battles of Lexington and Concord begin the American Revolution.

1776 The Declaration of Independence is signed. France and Spain give money to help the Americans fight Britain. Nathan Hale is captured by the British. He is charged with being a spy and is executed.

1777 Leaders choose a flag for America. The American troops win some important battles over the British. General Washington and his troops spend a very cold, hungry winter in Valley Forge.

1778 France sends ships to help the Americans win the war. The British are forced to leave Philadelphia.

1779 French ships head back to France. The French support the Americans in other ways.

1780 Americans discover that Benedict Arnold is a traitor. He escapes to the British. Major battles take place in North and South Carolina.

1781 The British surrender at Yorktown.

1783 A peace treaty is signed in France. British troops leave New York.

1787 The U.S. Constitution is written. Delaware becomes the first state in the Union.

1789 George Washington becomes the first president. John Adams is vice president.

FURTHER READING

Cook, Fred, adapter. *The Golden Book of the American Revolution* [adapted from *TheAmerican Heritage Book of the Revolution*]. New York: Golden Press, 1974.

Garrison, Webb. *Great Stories of the American Revolution.* Nashville, TN: Rutledge Hill Press, 1990.

Hall, Jonathan N. *Revolutionary War Quiz & Fact Book.* Dallas, TX: Taylor Publishing Company, 1999.

Kelly, C. Brian, et al. *Best Little Stories From the American Revolution.* Nashville, TN: Cumberland House, 1999.

Masoff, Joy. *American Revolution: 1700-1800.* New York: Scholastic Inc., 2000.

Wickwire, Franklin & Mary. *Cornwallis: The American Adventure.* Boston: Houghton Mifflin Company, 1970.

INDEX

Arnold, Benedict, 50

Brandywine Creek, Battle of, 30

Camden, Battle of, 34
Carolinas, 53-54, 59-60, 63, 66
    and Camden, 34
    and Charleston, 21-22, 23, 33-34,
        63, 66
    and Cowpens, 43-45
    and Guilford Court House,
        46-49
    and King's Mountain, 38-39
    and skirmishes, 36-37
Charleston, 21-22, 23, 33-34, 63, 66
Clare College, Cambridge, 10
Clinton, Henry, 21-23, 33-34, 49,
    50, 53, 54-56, 58, 62, 63, 68
Cornwallis, Lord Charles
    birth of, 7
    in British Army, 7, 10-15
    childhood of, 8-10
    children of, 18, 69
    in court of Prussian emperor, 68
    death of, 71
    education of, 8-10
    family of, 7-8, 15
    and lifestyle, 11-12
    as Marquis, 69
    and marriage, 17-18, 25, 30-32
    as official in France, 70
    in Parliament, 15, 17, 18
    as prisoner of war, 60, 68
    and Seven Years' War, 12-15
    and start of Revolution, 18-21
    and surrender at Yorktown, 7,
        60-63, 65-66, 68
    as viceroy of India, 68-69, 70-71
    as viceroy of Ireland, 69-70
Cowpens, Battle of, 43-45

De Choisy, Marquis, 59

De Grasse, Comte François Joseph
    Paul, 57-58, 59

Eton, 8-10

Ferguson, Patrick, 37, 38
France
    and American Revolution,
        32-33, 54, 56-59, 66
    Charles as official in, 70
    and Ireland, 70

Gates, Horatio, 34, 39
George III, King, 18-19, 36, 66
Greene, Nathanael, 39-40, 45, 46,
    48-49, 49, 53, 54
Guilford Court House, Battle at,
    46-49

Howe, William, 23

India, viceroy of, 68-69, 70-71
Ireland, viceroy of, 69-70

Jones, Jemima Tullekin (wife), 17-18,
    25, 30-32

King's Mountain, Battle at, 38-39

Lafayette, Marquis de, 54, 56, 58,
    59, 66
Lincoln, Benjamin, 34, 63
Long Island, New York, 24

Marion, Francis, 37
Monmouth Courthouse, Battle of,
    30
Morgan, Daniel, 44, 45

New Jersey, 24, 25, 26
    and Trenton, 26-27, 29, 30
New York, 23-24, 54-55, 66

North, Lord, 66

O'Hara, Charles, 46, 62, 63
Over-mountain men, 38

Paris, Treaty of, 67
Parliament, 15, 17, 18
Pickens, Andrew, 37

Rochambeau, Comte de, 56, 58

Seven Years' War, 12-15
Stamp Act of 1765, 18
Sumter, Thomas, 37

Tarleton, Banastre, 43-44, 59-60
Trenton, Battle of, 26-27, 29, 30

Virginia, 49, 53-56, 65-66
    See also Yorktown

Washington, George, 24, 25, 26, 29,
    39, 44, 55, 56, 58, 59, 60, 63, 66
Washington, William, 44
Wayne, Anthony, 54, 56
West Indies, 56-58

Yorktown, 51, 56, 58, 60
    surrender at, 7, 60-63, 65-66, 68

PICTURE CREDITS

ABOUT THE AUTHOR

DANIEL E. HARMON of Spartanburg, South Carolina, has written 29 books and numerous articles on topics ranging from history to humor. He is the editor of *The Lawyer's PC*, a national computer newsletter, and associate editor of *Sandlapper: The Magazine of South Carolina.*

Senior Consulting Editor **ARTHUR M. SCHLESINGER, JR.** is the leading American historian of our time. He won the Pulitzer Prize for his book *The Age of Jackson* (1945), and again for *A Thousand Days* (1965). This chronicle of the Kennedy Administration also won a National Book Award. He has written many other books, including a multi-volume series, *The Age of Roosevelt.* Professor Schlesinger is the Albert Schweitzer Professor of the Humanities at the City University of New York, and has been involved in several other Chelsea House projects, including the Colonial Leaders series of biographies on the most prominent figures of early American history.